Volume **4**   *Music for Millions*

World Famous

PIANO
CLASSICS

Edited by Hugo Frey

ISBN: 0-8256-4004-0

Consolidated Music Publishers, Inc.,   *33 West 60th Street, New York 10023*

$2.95

Contents by Titles

Contents by Composers

SLEEPING BEAUTY WALTZ

Arranged by
Hugo Frey

PETER TSCHAIKOWSKY

Moderate Waltz tempo

5

SWAN LAKE
THEME

PETER TSCHAIKOWSKY

VOCALISE

Op. 34, No. 14

Transcription by
Hugo Frey

SERGEI RACHMANINOFF

Lentamente e molto cantabile

ALLEGRETTO

from MOONLIGHT SONATA, Op. 27 No. 2

LUDWIG VAN BEETHOVEN

Allegretto D.C.

ADAGIO CANTABILE

from PATHETIQUE SONATA, Op. 13

LUDWIG van BEETHOVEN

MEDITATION

from "THAIS"

JULES MASSENET

Andante religioso

17

NARCISSUS

Op. 13, No. 4

ETHELBERT NEVIN

tranquillo

il basso una corda

THREE LITTLE PIECES

BELA BARTOK

Allegro robusto.

III

leggiero il basso

simile

AVE MARIA

FRANZ SCHUBERT

ANDANTE

from SONATA, Op. 26

LUDWIG van BEETHOVEN

ANDANTE CANTABILE

from the STRING QUARTET - Op. 11

Transcription by
Hugo Frey

PETER TSCHAIKOWSKY

Moderately slow

ROMEO AND JULIET

Theme from the OVERTURE

Transcription by
Hugo Frey

PETER TSCHAIKOWSKY

ARTISTS LIFE

JOHANN STRAUSS

INTRODUCTION
Andante moderato

36

INTERMEZZO

from "CAVALLERIA RUSTICANA"

PIETRO MASCAGNI

Andante

GOLD AND SILVER WALTZ

FRANZ LEHAR

No 1.

SALUT D'AMOUR

LOVE'S GREETING

EDWARD ELGAR

PIZZICATO POLKA

JOSEPH *and* JOHANN STRAUSS

47

EL CHOCLO

A. G. VILLOLDO

Moderato

EVENING PRAYER

from "HANSEL AND GRETEL"

ENGELBERT HUMPERDINCK

FANTAISIE-IMPROMPTU

FREDERIC CHOPIN

56

APPASSIONATA SONATA

Op. 57 — THEME

LUDWIG van BEETHOVEN

59

ARIA

from "THE MARRIAGE OF FIGARO"

WOLFGANG A. MOZART

March tempo

NEW WORLD SYMPHONY

LARGO

ANTON DVORAK

VALSE GRACIEUSE

ANTON DVORAK

O POLICHINELO

(PUNCHINELLO)

from PROLE DO BÉBÉ No. 1

H. VILLA-LOBOS

Presto

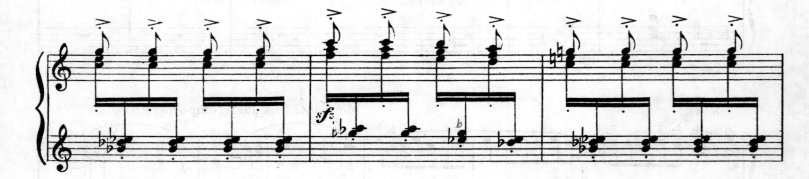

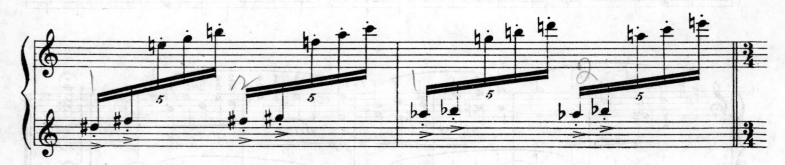

il canto distinto

PROLOGUE

from "I PAGLIACCI"

RUGGIERO LEONCAVALLO

LOVE-DEATH MUSIC

from "TRISTAN AND ISOLDE"

RICHARD WAGNER

75

76

ANDALUZA

PLAYERA — Op. 5 No. 5

ENRIQUE GRANADOS

Andantino quasi Allegretto

MARCH OF THE PRIESTS

from "ATHALIA"

FELIX MENDELSSOHN-BARTHOLDY

POLKA

from "THE BARTERED BRIDE"

BEDRICH SMETANA

Tempo di Polka

MAZURKA

Op. 7 No. 1

FREDERIC CHOPIN

ARIA

from "DON JUAN"

WOLFGANG A. MOZART

GLOCKENSPIEL

from "THE MAGIC FLUTE"

WOLFGANG A. MOZART

Allegro moderato

DREAMING

Op. 9 No. 4

RICHARD STRAUSS

GYMNOPEDIE No. 2

ERIK SATIE

Lent et trist

NOCTURNE

from "A MIDSUMMER NIGHT'S DREAM"

FELIX MENDELSSOHN

Andante espressivo

MARCH
from "LOVE OF THE THREE ORANGES"

SERGEI PROKOFIEFF

96

ORIENTALE

CESAR CUI

RUSTLE OF SPRING

CHRISTIAN SINDING

102

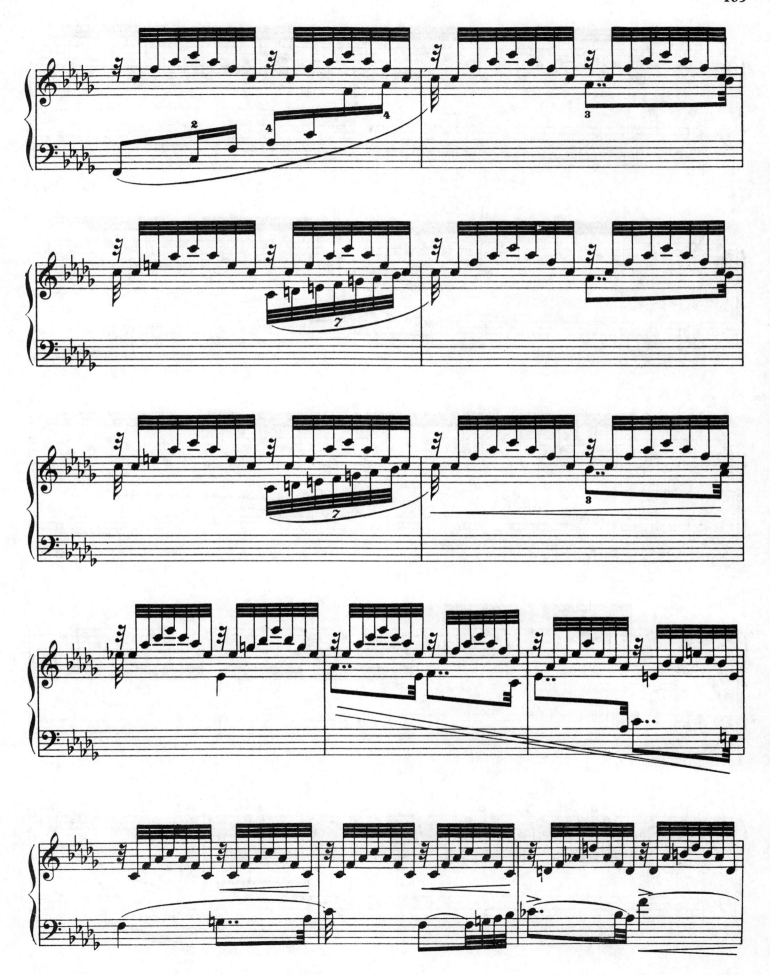

TRITSCH-TRATSCH POLKA

Op. 214

JOHANN STRAUSS

Made in U. S. A.

RONDE DES PRINCESSES

from "THE FIREBIRD"

IGOR STRAVINSKY

112

NORWEGIAN DANCE

Op. 35, No. 2

EDVARD GRIEG

Allegretto tranquillo e grazioso

Allegro

116

PRELUDE

Op. 28 No. 4

FREDERIC CHOPIN

MARCHE MILITAIRE

Op. 51 No. 1

FRANZ SCHUBERT

Trio

Marcia D.C. al Fine

TURKISH MARCH

from "RUINS OF ATHENS"

LUDWIG van BEETHOVEN

TO SPRING

Op. 43, No. 6

EDVARD GRIEG

FIFTH SYMPHONY
THEME - SECOND MOVEMENT

Transcription by
Hugo Frey

PETER TSCHAIKOWSKY

Andante cantabile *(slow)*

HAPPY HARLEQUIN

Paraphrased by
Domenico Savino

VICTOR HERBERT

EVENTIDE

Paraphrased by
Domenico Savino

VICTOR HERBERT

134

Appassionato

Tempo primo

PRELUDE IN G MINOR

Op. 23, No. 5

SERGEI RACHMANINOFF

Alla marcia. (♩ = 108.)

Un poco meno mosso.

Tempo I.

DANCE OF THE REED FLUTES

from "THE NUTCRACKER SUITE"

PETER TSCHAIKOWSKY

144

NOCTURNE No. 5

JOHN FIELD

TOCCATA

ARAM KHATCHATURIAN

Allegro marcatissimo ♩=120

149

154

Andante espressivo

A MEDIA LUZ

E. DONATO